About 3,0[illegible] ago in Israel, the boy who was to become King David was only in his early teens. He was the youngest of many brothers. His job was to tend sheep on his family's farm.

Next Reader, Please

War broke out between Israel and the Philistines. David's older brothers joined the army and went into battle. Young David stayed home with his father, but he would sometimes bring food to his brothers.

Next Reader, Please

The armies lined up on opposite sides of a valley and prepared to do battle. Just then, a Philistine warrior named Goliath came forward with an interesting challenge.

Next Reader, Please

Goliath offered to fight one warrior from Israel to decide the entire battle. The winning side would take over the land of the losing side. Do you think a war today could be decided so easily?

Next Reader, Please

So what do you think made Goliath so confident that he could beat any Israelite? Maybe it was that he was so big and strong. In fact, Goliath was over nine feet tall and wore over 100 pounds of armor!

Next Reader, Please

All of the men in Israel's army were afraid of this giant and would not come forward to fight. As Goliath waited for a challenger, David came up to the battle lines to bring food for his brothers.

Next Reader, Please

David saw Goliath defying the Israelites. This made him furious. David went to his king and told him that he wanted to fight Goliath. The king told David that he was just a boy and couldn't win.

Next Reader, Please

David told the king that God would give him strength to defeat the Philistine. He explained that God had helped him protect his father's sheep against bears and lions. David won the king's approval.

Next Reader, Please

David picked up his staff, sling and five stones and went to face the giant. When Goliath saw the boy, he mocked him and his humble weapons. Then Goliath described how he was going to kill David.

Next Reader, Please

David, however, had a weapon that Goliath didn't see. It was his faith in God. David took out one stone, put it in his sling and let it fly. Goliath was finished.

Next Reader, Please

When the Philistines saw what David had done to their champion, they turned and ran away. The Israelites were the victors. David grew up to become the King of Israel. He ruled for 40 years.

Next Reader, Please

King David married a woman named Bathsheba. They had a son named Solomon who would one day become a very wise king.

Next Reader, Please

David grew up to lead the Israelites. In what ways have you been a leader?

Of a group?
A family?
A company?
Anything else?

Next Reader, Please

David was the youngest of eight brothers. Did you have a lot of brothers and sisters?

Were you the youngest, oldest or in the middle?

Next Reader, Please

Did you or anyone in your family ever have a slingshot, BB gun or bow and arrow?

Were you a good shot?

Did you let your kids have these things?

Next Reader, Please

Have you ever faced a difficult challenge?

In sports?

Fighting a bully?

In a contest?

In other challenges?

Next Reader, Please

Did you know that David wrote many of the Psalms?

Do you know the rest of this Psalm?"

The LORD is my shepherd...
(I shall not want...)

Next Reader, Please

Thank you for reading and discussing this story!

Would you like to do this again some time?

Please pass your booklet to the leader.